PERSONAL GROWTH DIGEST

A COLLECTION OF GROWTH INSIGHTS

SWETA SINHA

BLUEROSE PUBLISHERS
India | U.K.

Copyright © Sweta Sinha 2025

All rights reserved by author. No part of this publication may be reproduced, stored in a retrieval system or transmitted in any form or by any means, electronic, mechanical, photocopying, recording or otherwise, without the prior permission of the author. Although every precaution has been taken to verify the accuracy of the information contained herein, the publisher assumes no responsibility for any errors or omissions. No liability is assumed for damages that may result from the use of information contained within.

BlueRose Publishers takes no responsibility for any damages, losses, or liabilities that may arise from the use or misuse of the information, products, or services provided in this publication.

For permissions requests or inquiries regarding this publication, please contact:

BLUEROSE PUBLISHERS
www.BlueRoseONE.com
info@bluerosepublishers.com
+91 8882 898 898
+4407342408967

ISBN: 978-93-7018-499-2

Cover design: Shubham Verma
Typesetting: Sagar

First Edition: April 2025

My Papa

Late S S Prasad.

(1956 to 1992)

To my beloved father,

Whom I lost 33 years ago when **I was just 8.**

Your absence became the deepest presence in my life. Though time stole your voice and touch, your strength, values, and love have silently shaped the person I am today.

This book is a tribute to your unseen guidance, your unspoken blessings, and the eternal bond that distance, time, and fate could never erase.

I carry you in every word, every lesson, and every dream fulfilled.

Forever your daughter,
Sweta

Foreword

As I sit down to write this foreword, I am filled with pride, love, and admiration for my sister, Sweta Sinha. Her remarkable journey, marked by resilience, determination, and courage, is an inspiration to me and countless others.

I was only two years old when our father passed away, and I don't have any memories of him. But my sister, who was 8 years at the time, had formed many fond memories with him. I can only imagine the devastating impact his loss must have had on her, especially at such a tender age. The pain and grief she endured are unfathomable to me, and yet, she survived and moved forward with remarkable strength and courage.

As we grew older, I witnessed my sister's transformation into a confident, smart, and compassionate individual. When she moved to Delhi, I was still in Dhanbad, pursuing my studies. I fondly remember her visits, which always brought joy and excitement. Her exposure to the big city had a profound impact on her, broadening her perspectives and shaping her into the person she is today.

Life had its share of challenges for my sister, including an engagement that didn't work out. However, she didn't let that setback define her. Instead, she moved forward, and her life took a beautiful turn when she married my wonderful brother-in-law. Together, they have built a life filled with love, laughter, and adventure.

I recall the days when my sister would travel to MBA college in a share auto, her sindoor-clad head held high. Today, she drives her own car to work, her hard-earned success. I couldn't be prouder.

One incident that left an indelible mark on me was when my sister interacted with an IAS officer during my wedding arrangements. Her confidence, poise, and articulate communication left everyone impressed.

As I look back, I realize that my sister has been my guiding light, my role model, and my best friend. From the little boy with two hair buns running behind her to school, I have grown into a person who deeply admires and respects her.

This book, Personal Growth Digest, is a culmination of my sister's life experiences, lessons learned, and insights gained. It's her resilience, courage, and determination. I have no doubt that her story will inspire, motivate, and transform the lives of countless readers.

I wish my sister all the best for this book and her future endeavors. I recommend Personal Growth Digest to everyone seeking guidance, comfort, or motivation. Thank you, Didi, for being a shining example of hope, courage, and triumph.

With love, admiration, and best wishes,

By Saurabh Sinha

Sweta—a name that embodies leadership, confidence, and inspiration. I have had the privilege of working alongside her for more than a decade across two organizations, and in that time, I have seen her transform not just her own career but also the lives of those around her. From her early days in business development to her role as Heading Customer Success Deaprtment, Sweta has always stood out as a determined, goal-oriented, and visionary professional.

What sets Sweta apart is her ability to lead with both strength and compassion. Her clarity of thought, confidence in decision-making, and unwavering dedication have made her a favorite among clients and colleagues alike. She doesn't just build relationships—she nurtures them, ensuring that success is not just an individual achievement but a shared journey.

Beyond her professional accomplishments, Sweta is a devoted mother, a supportive homemaker, and an inspiring mentor. I have had the opportunity to see her navigate both personal and professional challenges with remarkable grace, transforming every obstacle into an opportunity for growth. She is not just a leader in the workplace—she is a role model in life.

Her journey is a testament to resilience, ambition, and the power of believing in oneself. It is an honor to introduce this work, which reflects the wisdom, experiences, and insights of someone who has truly made a difference. I am confident that Sweta's work will inspire and empower every reader who comes across it.

By Ajendra Singh

Acknowledgment

This book is my dream project, and I am so happy to see it taking shape. My mantra—Dream, Believe, and Achieve—has truly worked!

No journey is ever walked alone, and mine has been blessed with remarkable people who have shaped me into who I am today.

First and foremost, my heartfelt gratitude to my Maa, Dev Rani Sinha, whose unwavering love and strength have been my foundation. To my brother, Saurabh Sinha, and Bhabhi, Shreelekha Anurag, for their constant support and belief in me. To my Badki Mausi and Badi Mummy, whose wisdom and affection have always guided me.

A special thank you to my husband, Ritesh, who has stood by me through every challenge, encouraging me to chase my dreams. To my kids, Nishtha and Shreshtha, who are my biggest inspiration and remind me every day of the power of love and purpose.

I am deeply grateful to my entire family—my paternal, maternal, and in-laws—who have supported me in countless ways throughout this journey.

To my colleagues, who have been my companions in growth and learning, and to my bosses, past and present, who have challenged and mentored me, helping me evolve both personally and professionally—thank you.

Each of you has played a part in my growth, and this book is a reflection of the lessons, love, and encouragement I have received along the way. I am truly grateful for your presence in my life and for being a part of my story.

From Sweta Sinha

Contents

Chapter 1: The Wheel of Life: Why It's Important to Follow for Personal Growth 1

Chapter 2: The different phases of Human Life 6

Chapter 3: Happiness & Sadness – Two Sides of the Same Coin 9

Chapter 4: The Hidden Iceberg: The Growing Mental Health Crisis 12

Chapter 5: The Universe is Always Working for You – But Are You Ready to Receive? 15

Chapter 6: The Importance of Prioritizing Personal Well-being 18

Chapter 7: Mastering Life's Curveballs: Lessons from a Roller Coaster Journey 20

Chapter 8: Happiness & Sadness – Two Sides of the Same Coin 24

Chapter 9: From Judgment to Triumph: A Journey of Strength, Sacrifice, and Self-Belief 27

Chapter 10: Knowing Isn't Enough: What Stops Us from Taking Action? 31

Chapter 11: The transformative powers of HCTm 34

Chapter 12: What Happens When You Analyze and Invest Just 10% of Your Time in Yourself? 38

Chapter 13: Greasy Mind vs Clear Thoughts:
            The case for daily Meditation 40

Chapter 14: The Power of Personal Responsibility:
            Taking Control of Our Lives............................ 42

Chapter 15: How Small Choices Shape
            Big Outcomes 45

Chapter 16: Embracing Change: The Key to
            Growth and Resilience 49

Chapter 17: Consistency is the Game: Play it Daily 55

Chapter 18: The Power of Small Steps: How the
            Compound Effect Transforms Your Life 57

Chapter 19: Aligning Life with Nature's Phases for a
            Healthier and Happier You 60

Chapter 20: The Power of Mind, Body, and Soul
            Alignment: A Journey to
            Holistic Health 62

Chapter 21: G Savers: My Daily Mantra
            for a Better Life 66

Chapter 22: The Alchemy of Self-Investment: A
            Transformative Journey 68

Chapter 23: The Power of Desire 70

Chapter 24; Be the Driver of your own Life!! 73

Chapter 25: Letting Go | An Art 75

Chapter 1

The Wheel of Life: Why It's Important to Follow for Personal Growth

The Wheel of Life is a powerful self-assessment tool that helps individuals evaluate and improve various areas of their lives. It serves as a visual representation of different life domains that contribute to overall well-being and fulfillment. By breaking down life into sections such as health, finances, career, relationships, and personal growth, the Wheel of Life provides a clear roadmap for balance and success.

What is the Wheel of Life?

The Wheel of Life consists of several segments, each representing a key aspect of life. These typically include:

1. Health: Your physical and mental well-being.
2. Finance: Your financial stability and goals.
3. Career: Your professional satisfaction and achievements.

4. Learning: Personal growth, education, and skills development.
5. Spirituality: Your sense of inner peace, faith, and connection to a higher purpose.
6. Social Connection: Your relationships with family, friends, and community.
7. Family: The bonds you share with your loved ones.
8. Dreams: Your personal aspirations, goals, and dreams for the future.

Each segment of the wheel represents an essential part of your life, and the goal is to assess where you stand in each area and work towards achieving harmony. When all the sections are balanced, the wheel rolls smoothly, symbolizing a fulfilled and happy life.

Why Is It Important to Follow the Wheel of Life?

1. Achieve Balance Across All Life Areas

One of the main reasons the Wheel of Life is so important is that it encourages balance. Life isn't just about work or finances; it's about making time for family, personal development, health, and dreams as well. Without balance, some areas of life may get neglected, leading to stress, dissatisfaction, or burnout. The Wheel of Life helps you maintain a balanced approach by giving you a visual overview of your priorities.

2. Clarify Your Priorities

When you use the Wheel of Life, you gain clarity about where you stand in each area. It helps you identify which areas are thriving and which need attention. By clearly seeing which life sections are underdeveloped or out of balance, you can focus your time and energy on what matters most. This allows you to prioritize areas that need improvement and set realistic goals to enhance your overall life satisfaction.

3. Increase Self-Awareness and Personal Growth

Self-awareness is a crucial element for personal growth. By regularly evaluating yourself using the Wheel of Life, you learn more about your strengths, weaknesses, desires, and challenges. This understanding empowers you to take actionable steps towards becoming a better version of yourself. The Wheel of Life helps you see the bigger picture of your life, allowing you to reflect on your progress and growth over time.

4. Stay Motivated and Goal-Oriented

The Wheel of Life provides a structured way to set and achieve goals in each area of life. By breaking down big goals into smaller, achievable tasks, you create momentum and motivation. As you see progress in one area, it encourages you to keep working on other areas, keeping you focused and motivated toward a well-rounded life.

5. Enhance Your Well-Being and Happiness

When all sections of the Wheel of Life are in balance, your overall well-being improves. A healthy balance in career, relationships, health, and personal development contributes to greater life satisfaction and happiness. The Wheel of Life reminds you to care for every aspect of yourself, promoting emotional, mental, and physical wellness.

6. Build Resilience in Difficult Times

By regularly evaluating and adjusting your life using the Wheel of Life, you build resilience. When challenges arise, you'll be better equipped to handle them because you've already identified areas of strength and areas that need more focus. If a particular section of your life is out of balance (for example, work-life imbalance or neglecting self-care), the Wheel of Life gives you the opportunity to adjust and re-focus before problems become overwhelming.

How to Use the Wheel of Life?

1. **Create Your Own Wheel:** Draw a circle and divide it into sections based on the key life areas you want to assess (health, career, finances, etc.).

2. **Evaluate Your Current State:** For each segment, rate your current satisfaction level from 1 (low) to 10 (high). This helps you see where you feel fulfilled and where you need more attention.

3. **Set Goals for Improvement:** Identify areas with lower ratings and create specific, measurable goals to improve them. For example, if your health score is low, you might set a goal to exercise regularly and eat a balanced diet.

4. **Review and Adjust:** The Wheel of Life is not static. It's an ongoing process that requires regular reflection and adjustment. Revisit it periodically to track progress and adjust goals as your needs and priorities change.

Conclusion

The Wheel of Life is an invaluable tool for personal development. By helping you assess different areas of your life and take action where necessary, it encourages balance, self-awareness, and growth. Following it allows you to design a life that is not only successful but also fulfilling, ensuring that you are living with purpose and happiness in all areas.

Chapter 2

The different phases of Human Life

For the past couple of days, a thought has been circling my mind: human lives are like a single day. The rise of the sun, its journey across the sky, and its eventual setting beautifully mirror the four distinct phases of our existence. This realization has given me a profound perspective on life and its fleeting yet meaningful journey.

Dawn (Childhood) 🌱

Just as the day begins with the gentle glow of sunrise, human life begins with the innocence and curiosity of childhood. This phase, spanning from **birth to around 12 years**, is full of wonder, learning, and boundless potential. The world is new and exciting, much like the first light of dawn revealing the landscape around us. We spend these years forming our personality, absorbing knowledge, and learning values. It's a time when the foundation for the rest of the day—or life—is laid, filled with playfulness and unrestrained joy.

Morning (Youth) ☀

As the sun climbs higher into the sky, it represents youth—the time of vibrancy, energy, and ambition. These are the years from **13 to 29,** when we dream big, take risks, and work tirelessly to shape our future. The morning light is bright but gentle, casting long shadows that remind us of the uncertainties we face while exploring our identity and place in the world. This phase is marked by exploration, boldness, and a sense of infinite possibility. It's the time to sow the seeds for the afternoon of life.

Afternoon (Adulthood) ☼

The afternoon marks the peak of the day—and life. As the sun shines brightest, adulthood is the phase of productivity, purpose, and responsibility. This phase, covering **30 to 59 years,** is when we are busiest, balancing careers, nurturing families, and striving for personal growth. The warmth of the afternoon sun symbolizes the fulfillment that comes from seeing the fruits of our labor. Stability and clarity dominate this phase as we work hard, not just for ourselves but for those who depend on us. It is a time of great achievement and significant contribution.

Evening & Dusk (Old Age) 🌆

As the day winds down and the sun begins its descent, we enter the evening of life. This phase, from **60 years onward**, is one of reflection, wisdom, and peace. The vibrant hues of dusk mirror the beauty of a life well-lived, filled with memories and lessons to share. It's a time to slow down, let go of the rush, and embrace tranquility. Just as the sunset signals the end of the day, old age reminds us of the impermanence of life and the importance of cherishing every moment. This is also a time to leave a legacy, passing on the torch to the next generation.

The Beauty of Every Phase

Viewing life as a single day helps us appreciate the unique charm of each phase. Every part of the day has its purpose—from the innocence of dawn to the vibrancy of morning, the productivity of the afternoon, and the peace of dusk. Each phase has its struggles and rewards, but together they form a complete, fulfilling journey.

So, wherever you are in the day of your life, pause and appreciate its beauty. Dawn, morning, afternoon, or dusk—each moment matters, and each phase contributes to the masterpiece of our existence. Let's honor the journey, embrace its impermanence, and make the most of the light while it lasts.

Chapter 3

Happiness & Sadness – Two Sides of the Same Coin

This morning, during my meditation, a thought crawled into my mind—happiness only holds meaning because we have tasted sadness. Without one, the other loses its value.

Yet, as we move through life, we often resist sadness, labeling it as something to be avoided, something "bad." We chase happiness relentlessly, believing it to be the ultimate goal. But what if happiness alone isn't enough? What if it only holds meaning because of its counterpart?

The Balance of Opposites

Imagine a life where you are always happy, where there is no sorrow, no struggle, no contrast. Would happiness still feel fulfilling? Or would it become mundane, just another default state of being?

The truth is, happiness and sadness exist in balance. Without night, we wouldn't appreciate the warmth of daylight. Without cold, we wouldn't cherish the comfort of warmth. The same applies to our emotions.

The depth of our sorrow expands our ability to experience true joy.

Think about the happiest moments of your life. Now ask yourself—would they feel as meaningful if you hadn't gone through hardship, heartbreak, or loss before them? It's the contrast that makes joy feel profound.

Why We Must Embrace Both

Society often conditions us to believe that sadness is something negative, something to be fixed or hidden. But sadness is not the enemy—it is a teacher. It slows us down, forces us to reflect, and deepens our understanding of ourselves and the world. Some of the most beautiful growth happens in our darkest moments.

When we fully accept both emotions as part of life's rhythm, we stop fearing sadness and start seeing it for what it is—a natural, necessary part of the human experience. We stop chasing happiness as an end goal and start appreciating it as a fleeting, yet beautiful, visitor.

A Reminder to Stay Present

We all know this truth deep inside, but in the noise of everyday life, we forget. That's why reiteration matters. That's why reminders are important—to bring us back to what's real.

So, the next time sadness visits, don't push it away. Let it be. Let it pass through you. And when happiness returns, welcome it with the same awareness. Because only when we've truly known both can we understand the depth of either.

Chapter 4

The Hidden Iceberg: The Growing Mental Health Crisis

Mental health has long been ignored, and today, it has become an iceberg—far deeper than what is visible on the surface. Anxiety, stress, and depression have become common in schools, colleges, workplaces, and homes, yet they are often overlooked. The consequences of neglecting mental well-being can be severe, affecting both individuals and society.

Understanding the Mental Health Crisis

Mental health encompasses emotional, psychological, and social well-being. It affects how we think, feel, and behave in daily life. However, due to societal stigma and lack of awareness, people often suppress their struggles, leading to silent suffering. The pressures of academic performance, career growth, financial burdens, and social expectations have made stress and anxiety a norm rather than an exception.

What Happens If Mental Health Is Ignored?

When mental health is left unaddressed, it can lead to:

- **Declining Productivity** – Stress and burnout reduce efficiency at work and school.

- **Physical Health Issues** – Chronic stress contributes to heart disease, obesity, and weakened immunity.

- **Strained Relationships** – Emotional instability affects personal and professional relationships.

- **Severe Mental Illness** – If left untreated, anxiety and depression can escalate into more severe conditions like suicidal tendencies or substance abuse.

How Can We Handle Mental Health Better?

- **Acknowledge and Talk About It** – Open conversations help in reducing stigma.

- **Seek Professional Help** – Therapy and counseling can provide the right guidance.

- **Adopt Healthy Lifestyle Choices** – Exercise, meditation, and proper sleep contribute to mental well-being.

- **Create Support Systems** – Schools, colleges, and workplaces should provide mental health programs.

- **Practice Self-Care** – Engaging in hobbies and taking breaks can help manage stress.

Conclusion

Mental health is not a luxury—it's a necessity. It's time we stop treating it as an afterthought and start addressing it proactively. By creating awareness, providing support, and encouraging open discussions, we can prevent this crisis from worsening. The deeper we dive into understanding mental health, the better we can navigate the iceberg before it causes irreversible damage.

Chapter 5

The Universe is Always Working for You – But Are You Ready to Receive?

Imagine this... The universe wants to overflow you with abundance – happiness, success, love, and peace. But the problem is that instead of standing with a **big bowl** to receive it, some people stand with a **small cup**. The blessings are right there, but they miss out because their mindset limits what they can receive.

I know someone who's going through this. God has given him everything – a loving family, good health, and opportunities – but he's stuck in a loop of blame, complaints, and ego. Instead of taking responsibility and making efforts, he's letting everything slip away from his hands.

I often wonder why people behave like this. After observing closely, I found three key reasons behind this destructive attitude:

♣ 3 Reasons Why People Sabotage Their Own Blessings

1. Fixed Mindset & Lack of Gratitude

People with a fixed mindset believe life is unfair to them. They constantly compare themselves to others and fail to appreciate what they already have. They think they deserve more but never stop to be thankful for what's already there.

2 Playing the Blame Game

Instead of taking responsibility, they blame their circumstances, fate, or even their family. This keeps them stuck in the same place, as they never reflect on their own actions or make efforts to change things.

3.Arrogance & Ego

Arrogance blinds them from seeing the truth. They reject advice, dismiss opportunities, and think they know it all. Ego creates distance from loved ones and isolates them from the blessings that life offers.

💡 How to Change This Mindset

1. Practice Gratitude Daily:

Shift the focus from what's missing to what's already there. Gratitude brings clarity and positivity, making you more open to receiving abundance.

2. Take Personal Responsibility:

Stop blaming others. Start asking yourself, "What can I do to improve my situation?" Accountability is the first step toward transformation.

3. Stay Humble & Open to Learning:

Humility is key to growth. Accept that you don't know everything and be willing to learn from others. Ego blocks blessings, but humility opens new doors.

Final Thought:

Life gives everyone opportunities, but it's up to us to be mindful and open enough to receive them. Don't stand with a small cup – bring a big bowl and welcome abundance with gratitude, responsibility, and humility.

In today's fast-paced world, we often chase success, wealth, and external achievements, yet we tend to overlook one of the most crucial aspects of a fulfilling life—**our health.** It is high time we recognize that a successful life is incomplete without good health. Personal well-being should be at the top of our priority list, but unfortunately, it is often the most neglected.

Chapter 6

The Importance of Prioritizing Personal Well-being

Our quality of life is directly impacted by our **physical and mental health.** Whether we are battling lifestyle diseases such as **high blood pressure and diabetes** or simply feeling fatigued and uninspired, our well-being influences our ability to be productive and creative. Instead of creating something meaningful, many of us end up complaining about our deteriorating health.

Each one of us is given the same **24 hours in a day**. After sleeping for about eight hours, we are left with sixteen waking hours. Devoting just one hour daily to self-care can significantly improve our quality of life. Yet, many people fail to take this small yet powerful step toward a healthier lifestyle. The lack of awareness and effort in personal well-being is alarming. Why are people **not investing in their self-improvement journey?** The answer often lies in laziness and misplaced priorities. Instead of taking charge of our own health, **we tend to blame others or external circumstances for our fate.**

Being physically and mentally fit is not just a choice; **it is a necessity.** If we neglect our health, we will eventually find ourselves bedridden, dependent on doctors, and spending our hard-earned money on medical bills. **The reality is that healthcare professionals and the pharmaceutical industry thrive because we fail to take responsibility for our well-being.** At the very least, every household should **adopt a basic health routine.** Parents must instill discipline in their children so that future generations grow up prioritizing health and wellness.

If we fail to make this shift, we will continue to face an epidemic of obesity, high blood pressure, diabetes, stress, anxiety, and poor decision-making. The key to true transformation lies in returning to the basics— **regular exercise, mindful eating, mental relaxation, and overall self-care.** This is the best gift we can offer ourselves, our children, and future generations. A healthier society starts with healthier individuals, and it is time we take this responsibility seriously.

Chapter 7

Mastering Life's Curveballs: Lessons from a Roller Coaster Journey

Life has never been a straight, smooth flight for me. It has been a thrilling roller coaster—full of unexpected turns, sharp drops, and moments where I wasn't sure if I'd scream in excitement or sheer panic. Just when I thought I had things figured out, life threw me another curveball. And then another.

At first, I struggled. I tried to **catch every single challenge** that came my way, often feeling overwhelmed. But with time, I learned that not every ball needs to be caught, and not every setback is a failure. Through my experiences, I've picked up valuable lessons that I believe can help anyone navigating their own unpredictable journey.

1. Not Every Ball Needs to Be Caught 🎯

Early on, I used to believe I had to chase every opportunity, fix every problem, and respond to every challenge. But the truth is, some curveballs are meant to be *let go*.

- ♦ You don't have to win every argument.

- ♦ You don't have to accept every opportunity.

- ♦ You don't have to fix everything for everyone.

Instead of trying to juggle everything, focus on what truly matters. Choose your battles wisely. Some balls are best left to roll away.

2. Adaptability Is the Secret Superpower ☐ ♂

Life doesn't play fair. It doesn't give you a warning before throwing something unexpected your way. The key to thriving is ***adaptability.***

I learned to catch curveballs in different ways—sometimes by jumping, rolling, or simply shifting my stance. The same applies to life:

- ✅ If one strategy isn't working, try another.

- ✅ Be flexible with your approach but firm with your goals.

- ✅ When things don't go as planned, don't freeze—adjust.

Resilience isn't just about standing strong; it's about bending without breaking.

3. You'll Drop Some Balls—And That's Okay! 🙈 ♂

Let's be honest—there were many moments when I simply couldn't keep up. I dropped the ball, missed opportunities, or made mistakes. In the past, I used to chase after these lost chances, feeling regret and frustration. But here's what I realized:

⊘ *You don't have to win at everything to succeed in life.*

⊘ *Perfection is an illusion; progress is real.*

The best thing you can do is learn from the misses, shake off the losses, and prepare for the next challenge.

4. Focus on Who You're Becoming, Not Just What's Happening 🚀

At some point, I stopped asking *"Why is this happening to me?"* and started asking *"What is this teaching me?"*

Challenges, setbacks, and surprises are all shaping us into who we are meant to be. Instead of obsessing over controlling every outcome, focus on the person you are becoming through these experiences.

💡 Are you growing stronger?

💡 Are you learning patience?

💡 Are you becoming more resilient?

That's where the real magic happens.

5. Enjoy the Game, Even When It Gets Tough 🌀

At the end of the day, life is a game. You will catch some wins, miss some opportunities, and laugh at a few unexpected surprises. Don't take it too seriously. Enjoy the journey, laugh at your mistakes, and trust that you are exactly where you need to be.

If life is throwing you curveballs, take a deep breath, stay focused, and play along. You never know—you just might hit a home run.

Final Thoughts

No matter how unpredictable life gets, remember: every challenge is an opportunity in disguise. The more you embrace uncertainty, the more you grow. So here's to catching, dodging, and rolling with whatever comes next!

What's one curveball life threw at you that ended up teaching you a valuable lesson? Drop your thoughts in the comments! Let's learn from each other.

Chapter 8

Happiness & Sadness – Two Sides of the Same Coin

This morning, during my meditation, a thought crawled into my mind—happiness only holds meaning because we have tasted sadness. Without one, the other loses its value.

Yet, as we move through life, we often resist sadness, labeling it as something to be avoided, something "bad." We chase happiness relentlessly, believing it to be the ultimate goal. But what if happiness alone isn't enough? What if it only holds meaning because of its counterpart?

The Balance of Opposites

Imagine a life where you are always happy, where there is no sorrow, no struggle, no contrast. Would happiness still feel fulfilling? Or would it become mundane, just another default state of being?

The truth is, happiness and sadness exist in balance. Without night, we wouldn't appreciate the warmth of daylight. Without cold, we wouldn't cherish the comfort of warmth. The same applies to our emotions.

The depth of our sorrow expands our ability to experience true joy.

Think about the happiest moments of your life. Now ask yourself—would they feel as meaningful if you hadn't gone through hardship, heartbreak, or loss before them? It's the contrast that makes joy feel profound.

Why We Must Embrace Both

Society often conditions us to believe that sadness is something negative, something to be fixed or hidden. But sadness is not the enemy—it is a teacher. It slows us down, forces us to reflect, and deepens our understanding of ourselves and the world. Some of the most beautiful growth happens in our darkest moments.

When we fully accept both emotions as part of life's rhythm, we stop fearing sadness and start seeing it for what it is—a natural, necessary part of the human experience. We stop chasing happiness as an end goal and start appreciating it as a fleeting, yet beautiful, visitor.

A Reminder to Stay Present

We all know this truth deep inside, but in the noise of everyday life, we forget. That's why reiteration matters. That's why reminders are important—to bring us back to what's real.

So, the next time sadness visits, don't push it away. Let it be. Let it pass through you. And when happiness returns, welcome it with the same awareness. Because only when we've truly known both can we understand the depth of either.

Chapter 9

From Judgment to Triumph: A Journey of Strength, Sacrifice, and Self-Belief

Fourteen years ago, I made a decision that would forever change my life. A decision that, at the time, felt more like a necessity than a choice. My daughter, just 1.5 years old, was at the center of my world, but I was also at a crossroads. I needed more—not just for her, but for myself. I craved a sense of purpose, financial independence, and a name of my own.

Stepping out of the home and into the corporate world was not easy. It was a leap of faith. But when I cracked that first interview and landed my first job, I knew it was the beginning of something monumental.

The Weight of Judgment

Back then, the world was quick to judge. Relatives and friends looked at me with disapproval, often calling me "cold-hearted" for leaving my baby at home while I worked. The guilt was suffocating. Many believed that a mother's place should be at home, nurturing her child at every moment. I couldn't help but feel the sting of their words.

It wasn't just about leaving my daughter; it was about pursuing a dream that had been placed on hold for years. I was told that a good mother prioritizes her child above all else—*and I did*. But I also knew that for me to give her the best, I had to start by giving myself the best.

Overcoming the Guilt

But no matter how harsh the judgments were, one thing remained clear: I had a purpose. People will always have something to say—it's their job. But, ultimately, it was my journey, and I couldn't let their words define it.

I found solace in an old Hindi song, *"Kuchh toh log kahenge, logon ka kaam hai kehna."* And in those moments of doubt, I'd remind myself, *"Tujhko chalna hoga, tujh chalna hoga."* I had to walk, and walk I did.

A Transformative Journey

The journey was anything but easy. The first years were filled with long hours, tough decisions, and a constant juggling act between career and family. There were days when I felt torn, moments when I wondered if I had made the right choice. But then there were moments of victory—small, yet powerful—when I saw the fruits of my hard work: financial independence, a sense of accomplishment, and, most importantly, growth.

Today, when I look back, I see how far I've come. Not just in terms of career success but in my personal growth as a mother, a woman, and an individual. I've built a name for myself, gained confidence, and, most importantly, learned that true fulfillment comes from balancing both my personal and professional life.

A Change in Perception

The same people who once judged me now look at me with pride. Some have even confessed, "I wish I had done what you did. I wish I had worked or taken steps toward financial freedom." It's a humbling feeling to hear these words, but it's also a reminder that our journeys are not always understood in the moment, but they are often admired later on.

A Message for All the Dreamers

To all the women out there who may feel guilty for chasing their dreams or pursuing a career while raising a family—remember this: People will say what they will, but their opinions do not define you. Your path is yours alone. And the journey will be worth every challenge, every sacrifice, and every moment of doubt.

You may be questioned, you may be judged, but at the end of the day, your resilience, your determination, and your courage to pursue your dreams will speak louder than any criticism.

If you ever feel overwhelmed, let the words of that song resonate in your heart, and keep walking, because *"tujhko chalna hoga"*. You have to keep going. The road may be difficult, but the destination is more beautiful than you could ever imagine.

Conclusion: Redefining Success

Looking back, I don't see the sacrifices as losses. They were investments. They were the foundation upon which I've built my life—one where my career and family coexist harmoniously. The same people who once questioned me now look at the life I've created with admiration. And to all the women who are just beginning their journey—I see you. Your dreams are valid. You deserve to pursue them.

Because at the end of the day, success isn't about what others think. It's about what you've achieved, who you've become, and the lives you've touched along the way. Your journey will inspire others, and more importantly, it will give you the strength to keep walking toward the life you deserve.

Key Takeaways:

- *Chase your dreams, even when it feels impossible or when people doubt you.*

- *Judgment will come, but it is your journey that matters the most.*

- *Keep moving forward—because your success will be your answer to the world's questions.*

Chapter 10

Knowing Isn't Enough: What Stops Us from Taking Action?

We live in an age of abundant information. We know what's right for our health, career, and relationships. We know we should exercise, eat healthy, save money, or work towards our goals. But how often do we actually act on this knowledge? The truth is, many of us remain stuck in a loop of knowing but not doing.

Why does this happen? Why do we hesitate to take that one small action that could transform our lives?

1. Fear of Failure

One of the biggest barriers is the fear of failing. What if we try and don't succeed? This thought paralyzes us, leading to procrastination. We prefer the comfort of our current state over the risk of disappointment.

2. Overthinking

The more we think, the less we act. We analyze every detail, consider every possible outcome, and get overwhelmed by "what-ifs." This mental exhaustion kills the momentum to start.

3. Lack of Confidence

Doubt often whispers, "Am I good enough? What if I'm not ready?" This lack of belief in ourselves stops us from stepping out of our comfort zones.

4. Procrastination

We tell ourselves, "Tomorrow will be better; I'll start then." Days turn into weeks, and weeks into months, while we keep postponing what matters most.

5. Unclear Priorities

Sometimes, we don't act because we aren't sure what truly matters. Without clear goals, we drift aimlessly, doing what's easy instead of what's necessary.

6. Perfectionism

Waiting for the "perfect moment" is another trap. We think everything must align before we act, but in reality, perfection rarely exists.

The Cost of Inaction

Every time we delay action, we pay a price: opportunities lost, dreams delayed, and self-doubt strengthened. Knowing without action creates a gap that leads to frustration.

How to Overcome This?

Start Small: A single step is better than no step at all. Break tasks into tiny actions and focus on one at a time.

Embrace Imperfection: Done is better than perfect. Take action even if it's not flawless.

Remind Yourself of the "Why": Reflect on why you want this change. A strong reason fuels motivation.

Use Accountability: Share your goals with someone who will push you to stay committed.

Act Despite Fear: Fear will always exist, but courage is taking action anyway.

Final Thoughts

Knowing gives you potential, but action turns that potential into reality. The next time you hesitate, ask yourself: What's the worst that could happen? And what's the best that could happen if I just try? Often, you'll find the best is worth the risk.

Chapter 11

The transformative powers of HCTm

I recently watched a video of Akshay Kumar delivering a speech about the three principles that have led to his success and made him stand out from the crowd. He spoke about three fundamental disciplines: mastering habits, practicing punctuality and time management, and maintaining consistency. He emphasized that anyone who incorporates these principles into their daily life is bound to achieve success. Inspired by his words, I reflected on my own journey and realized how these principles have transformed my life.

The Power of Habits, Consistency, and Time Management

Success in life is not a matter of luck but a product of disciplined effort and structured habits. These three principles—**habits, consistency, and time management**—are the cornerstones of achieving greatness. When embraced, they have the power to transform lives. Let's delve into each of them and understand how they can guide anyone to success.

1. Habits: The Building Blocks of Success

Habits are small, regular actions that shape your daily routine. They are the foundation of how you spend your time and energy. Good habits, when cultivated, create positive momentum in life. For example:

- Exercising daily keeps your body healthy.
- Reading regularly expands your knowledge.
- Meditating calms your mind and enhances focus.

Habits work because they automate actions, saving mental energy for more significant decisions. To develop good habits, start small and stay consistent. For instance, if you want to read, commit to just 5 minutes daily. Over time, this grows into a powerful routine.

2. Consistency: The Power of Showing Up Daily

Consistency is about showing up and putting in the effort every day, no matter how small. It is not the occasional big effort but the regular, smaller ones that lead to remarkable results. This principle leverages the compounding effect: small efforts repeated over time lead to exponential growth.

For example:

- Writing one page a day can result in a book within a year.
- Practicing a skill for 30 minutes daily can make you proficient over time.

Consistency builds trust—with yourself and others. It shows that you are reliable and disciplined, which is crucial in personal and professional relationships.

3. Time Management: Mastering the 24 Hours

We all have 24 hours in a day, but how we use them determines our success. Time management is the art of prioritizing tasks and eliminating distractions to focus on what truly matters. Effective time management includes:

- **Planning:** Start each day with a clear plan of your priorities.

- **Eliminating distractions:** Turn off unnecessary notifications and create a focused workspace.

- **Batching tasks:** Group similar tasks together to save time.

Learning to say "no" to unimportant tasks is also crucial. By managing your time well, you can achieve more without feeling overwhelmed.

Transforming Lives with These Principles

When these three principles are combined, they create a powerful framework for success. Akshay Kumar, a renowned actor, attributes his success to mastering these practices. By focusing on habits, staying consistent, and managing time effectively, he has reached the pinnacle of his career.

Personally, I have experienced a profound transformation by adopting these principles. Earlier, despite having 24 hours in a day, I often felt stuck and unproductive. Now, by mastering my habits, showing up daily, and managing my time wisely, my life has changed. People often ask me, "What's your secret?" The answer is simple: it's the power of discipline, consistency, and time management.

The Compounding Effect

The magic lies in the compounding effect. Small, consistent efforts add up over time to create extraordinary results. Whether it's improving your health, building a career, or nurturing relationships, the principles of habits, consistency, and time management will guide you toward success.

Final Thoughts

Success is within everyone's reach. By focusing on building strong habits, staying consistent, and managing your time effectively, you can transform your life. Start small, remain patient, and trust the process—the results will amaze you.

Chapter 12

What Happens When You Analyze and Invest Just 10% of Your Time in Yourself?

Have you ever wondered where your time really goes? I decided to analyze how I spent my time in 2024, and the results were eye-opening.

Here's what the data revealed:

- zzz **33% of my time** went to sleeping (a non-negotiable).

- 🖥 **30% of my time** was dedicated to working.

- 🛒 **25% of my time** was consumed by miscellaneous activities—errands, chores, and everyday tasks.

- And yet, with just **10% of my time**, I focused on *myself*.

What did I do with that 10%? 🌿 **Meditation**: 15 minutes a day gave me calmness, clarity, and focus. 📚 **Reading Books**: 30 minutes daily helped me expand my horizons, dream bigger, and shift my mindset.

Pooja Path: Staying connected to my spirituality kept me grounded and intentional. 🕉 **Learning New Skills**: Pursuing my passion for Kathak and professional growth brought immense joy and achievement.

🌟 **Here's What That 10% Achieved:**

- I fulfilled dreams I once thought were impossible.

- I gained clarity, confidence, and focus in both personal and professional life.

- I found balance and purpose in every aspect of my day-to-day living.

The Data Speaks for Itself: If 90% of my time was spent on work, sleep, and daily essentials, it was this intentional 10% that created the *real* transformation.

💡 **The Takeaway:** Self-improvement doesn't need all your time—it just needs a small, consistent slice of it. Imagine what you could achieve if you invested just 10% of your year in activities that nurture your growth.

The numbers don't lie. Your growth is waiting—start analyzing, start investing, and watch your life change.

Chapter 13

Greasy Mind vs Clear Thoughts: The case for daily Meditation

Meditation is a powerful tool for clarity, peace, and mindfulness. However, my personal experience has taught me an important lesson: the true benefits of meditation come with consistency. If you skip meditation for a week or lose the rhythm, you may have to pay the price.

When meditation is paused, I notice the following:

Irritation: Small things start bothering me more than they should.

Confusion: Decision-making becomes harder, and second-guessing grows.

Mental Fog: My thoughts feel heavy and unclear, like a cloudy sky.

It's as if the mind becomes greasy, slippery, and cluttered. To clean it, one needs the **metaphorical "scrubber" of focused meditation and effort.** But the process of regaining that clarity and stillness takes time and patience.

This experience has shown me that maintaining a daily meditation practice is like maintaining personal hygiene for the mind. Just as we wouldn't skip brushing our teeth or showering, meditation should be seen as essential maintenance for our mental well-being.

Key Takeaways for Consistency:

1. Prioritize Your Practice: Treat meditation as a non-negotiable part of your day.

2. Start Small, Stay Steady: Even 10 minutes daily is better than skipping entirely.

3. Forgive Yourself: If you slip up, don't dwell on it—just restart.

4. Observe the Difference: Reflect on how meditation influences your mental clarity and emotions.

Meditation doesn't just happen; it requires commitment. **It's a continuous journey of effort** and reward. Consistency not only prevents the "greasy mind" but also strengthens our ability to handle life's challenges with grace and balance.

So, let's embrace this journey with discipline and remember that a clear, fog-free mind is worth the effort!

Chapter 14

The Power of Personal Responsibility: Taking Control of Our Lives

Personal responsibility is more than just a concept; it is the key to shaping our lives and our future. It's about understanding that our actions, decisions, and attitudes directly impact the world around us. When we take responsibility for ourselves, we empower not only our own lives but also the lives of those around us.

Why is it important?

1. It Helps Us Grow

Every choice we make teaches us something. By taking responsibility for our actions, we become more aware of the consequences, both good and bad. This awareness helps us grow. Mistakes are a part of life, but when we own them, we learn from them and become better, stronger versions of ourselves.

2. It Builds Trust

When we take responsibility, we show others that they can rely on us. Trust is the foundation of any relationship, whether personal or professional. By being accountable for our words and actions, we create an environment where honesty, respect, and reliability can thrive.

3. It Increases Our Freedom

It may seem counterintuitive, but taking responsibility actually brings us more freedom. When we own our choices, we can steer our lives in the direction we desire. We are no longer victims of circumstance but active creators of our own path. The more we take control of our actions, the less we are controlled by the world around us.

4. It Creates a Positive Impact

When each one of us takes responsibility for our actions, we begin to see the ripple effect. Small changes in the way we think, and act can inspire others to do the same. By owning our decisions, we contribute to a world where personal integrity and respect are valued above all.

How can we practice personal responsibility?

Be Honest with ourselves about our mistakes and our growth.

Own Your Choices: Remember, we are the creators of our story.

Learn from Your Actions: Take time to reflect on both successes and failures.

Be Consistent in showing up for yourself and others.

Personal responsibility is not about perfection. It's about progress and understanding that we are accountable for the lives we live. Let's choose to take responsibility, not as a burden, but as a gift that allows us to live with purpose, integrity, and freedom.

As we take control of our own lives, we help shape a world where each individual's actions contribute to a brighter, more connected future.

Embrace personal responsibility—own your life, and see the change it brings.

Chapter 15

How Small Choices Shape Big Outcomes

The morning after Diwali and Chhath Puja is often a blend of celebration and lingering holiday fatigue. For many of us, this period marks a return to routine, sometimes without the support we rely on. For me, this particular morning felt like an uphill climb. With my mom away, the usual helping hands weren't there, and it was up to me to get the kids ready for school, manage the house, and find my own focus. As soon as I woke up, I felt a wave of tiredness—a signal that if I didn't take control of my mindset, my entire day (or even week) could suffer.

Thankfully, our maid was there to help—a blessing, but one that made a difference. Yet, despite this, I knew that my energy and mindset would determine how the day unfolded. So, when that first wave of sluggishness hit, I paused, took a deep breath, and silently repeated to myself, "I can do it!" three times. I let each affirmation build upon the last, and something shifted. Those words carried a surprising power, pulling me out of my initial low energy and putting me in charge of my day.

Why Self-Work Matters in Everyday Moments

The experience was a reminder of why self-work is so crucial. Over time, I've learned that working on my mindset is like planting seeds; it may take time, but when those seeds bloom, they provide strength in unexpected ways. If I hadn't been investing in personal growth, I might have let negative thoughts and fatigue take over. Instead, I found resilience within, turning a potentially difficult day into one of productivity and positivity.

Working on yourself is like building an inner toolkit. You may not need every tool every day, but when the need arises, those tools are ready. Today, my tools were resilience, positive affirmations, and the belief that I could handle whatever the day brought.

Small Morning Choices, Big Daily Impact

Each morning is a new canvas, and our actions determine what gets painted on it. Taking a moment to affirm my ability to handle the day shifted the tone not only for that day but also for the week ahead. If I'd let negativity take over, I could have spent the whole day feeling overwhelmed. Instead, I chose positivity, and that small choice set a ripple effect in motion.

Whether it's starting the day with a mantra, a few minutes of meditation, or simply a positive affirmation, these small practices can be transformative. They don't necessarily change the tasks at hand, but they change how we approach them. And that difference—how we show up—is everything.

Why Every Day is a New Opportunity

It's easy to get caught up in life's challenges, especially in times when responsibilities weigh heavily. But no matter what our circumstances look like, each day offers a fresh start, a blank slate on which we can paint our mood, goals, and intentions. When we wake up with this mindset, we empower ourselves to choose positivity over doubt, resilience over fatigue.

Today's choice reminded me of the value of self-investment. Each time we choose to work on ourselves, to believe in our own resilience, we're creating an inner foundation. This foundation supports us when we face challenges, like busy mornings or unexpected setbacks. It helps us shape not only our own day but the energy we bring to those around us.

Practical Tips to Start Your Day Strong

1. **Use Affirmations**: Just a few moments of positive affirmations, like saying "I can do it," can set a strong tone. Repeating these words—even silently—can have a powerful impact on your mindset.

2. **Take Small Steps**: Instead of overwhelming yourself with everything on your plate, break

it down. Focus on completing one task at a time. These small steps build momentum.

3. **Acknowledge Small Blessings**: Recognizing and appreciating little things, like support from others, can create a positive mindset. It reminds us that even on tough days, there's something to be grateful for.

4. **Set an Intention**: Setting a simple intention for the day helps create focus and gives you a guiding light. Whether it's "Today, I'll stay calm," or "Today, I'll be productive," your intention helps shape your actions.

5. **Celebrate Wins, Big or Small**: Acknowledge your efforts, even if it's just showing up and giving it your best. Self-recognition builds confidence and keeps you motivated.

Final Thoughts: The Power of Small Changes

Each morning is a chance to reset, to step forward with positivity, and to make small choices that shape big outcomes. By investing in ourselves, we're creating the inner resilience that shows up when we need it most. Today was a reminder that self-work is not just about grand goals but about the small ways we choose to show up every day.

So, here's to starting each day with a fresh mindset and to realizing that every day is a blank canvas. It's up to us to fill it with the colors of resilience, gratitude, and purpose. Keep working on yourself—because when life's challenges arise, the strength you've cultivated will be ready to support you.

Chapter 16

Embracing Change: The Key to Growth and Resilience

Change is one of the few constants in life, yet, ironically, it's something many of us instinctively resist. We build comfort zones—safe, familiar spaces where we feel secure and at ease. However, while these comfort zones can offer a sense of stability, staying within them for too long can lead to stagnation. Growth, after all, rarely happens in comfort. To truly thrive in life, we need to adopt a growth mindset, one that welcomes change rather than resists it. Here, we'll explore why accepting change is essential, how a growth mindset can help us navigate it, and practical ways to step outside our comfort zones.

The Pitfalls of Resisting Change

When we resist change, life becomes increasingly difficult. Think about it: every major milestone, career shift, or personal evolution requires us to let go of old habits, beliefs, or routines to make way for something new. Yet, if we refuse to accept these changes, we find ourselves stuck, clinging to outdated ways that may no longer serve us. Resistance creates friction, which, over time, can turn into stress, frustration, and a lack of fulfillment.

Holding on to a fixed mindset—a belief that our abilities and circumstances are set in stone—exacerbates this challenge. People with a fixed mindset see change as threatening because it challenges their established sense of self and stability. They see setbacks or new situations as obstacles rather than opportunities, making them more likely to shy away from situations that push them out of their comfort zones. As a result, they may miss out on potential growth, career advancements, and richer relationships.

The Power of a Growth Mindset

On the other hand, adopting a growth mindset—the belief that we can develop our abilities and adapt over time—empowers us to embrace change. People with a growth mindset view challenges as opportunities to learn, grow, and evolve. Rather than fearing the unknown, they see it as a pathway to potential.

To cultivate a growth mindset, it's important to:

1. **See Failure as Feedback**: Instead of fearing failure, treat it as a valuable lesson. Failures are steppingstones to future success and teach us what doesn't work, so we can get closer to what does.

2. **Challenge Limiting Beliefs**: Often, our greatest barriers to change are beliefs we hold about ourselves, such as "I'm not good at this" or "This isn't for me." Question these beliefs—are they facts, or just assumptions based on past experiences?

3. **Embrace Lifelong Learning**: View every day as an opportunity to learn something new. The more we learn, the better equipped we are to face life's inevitable changes with confidence and resilience.

Comfort Zones: Our Safe Place... or a Trap?

Our comfort zone gives us a sense of control, stability, and safety. However, staying within this zone for too long can lead to rigidity. Imagine muscles that are never stretched—they become tight and inflexible, and the same happens with our minds when we refuse to stretch our thinking or try new things. Rigidity, in this sense, is the enemy of resilience.

Over time, remaining in the comfort zone dulls our ability to adapt and respond to changes. We end up withholding ourselves from the very experiences that could enrich our lives and make us stronger. By avoiding challenges, we miss out on personal and professional growth and the opportunity to develop new skills or gain fresh perspectives.

The Consequences of Resisting Change

Resisting change doesn't just limit personal growth—it can create a significant emotional toll. Holding tightly to the way things "should" be, rather than accepting the way things "are," can lead to constant frustration, anxiety, and a sense of powerlessness. The more we push back against life's inevitable shifts, the harder it becomes to deal with new circumstances. This resistance can lead to:

- **Increased Stress**: Constantly fighting against change is exhausting and can lead to mental and emotional burnout.

- **Reduced Resilience**: When we avoid discomfort, we miss out on the opportunity to build resilience, a crucial trait for navigating life's ups and downs.

- **Missed Opportunities**: Resisting change can prevent us from pursuing exciting opportunities, whether it's a new job, a meaningful relationship, or a lifestyle improvement.

Steps to Embrace Change and Step Outside the Comfort Zone

If we want to live a fulfilling life, we must learn to face and accept change. Here are some practical ways to begin:

1. **Take Small Steps**: You don't have to overhaul your entire life at once. Start by

making small, manageable changes. It could be as simple as trying a new hobby, changing up your routine, or meeting new people. Small steps build confidence and make bigger changes feel less intimidating.

2. **Practice Mindfulness**: When you start to feel resistant, pause and observe your thoughts. Mindfulness can help you recognize when fear or discomfort is holding you back, allowing you to make conscious choices rather than reacting automatically.

3. **Seek Out New Experiences**: Push yourself to try new things regularly. Exposure to new experiences helps reduce the fear of the unknown and strengthens your adaptability. Even seemingly small shifts, like exploring a new city or taking a different route to work, can broaden your perspective.

4. **Surround Yourself with a Positive Support System**: People who encourage growth, motivate you, and provide constructive feedback make it easier to embrace change. Being around those who have a growth mindset helps normalize change and reduce fear.

5. **Celebrate Progress, Not Perfection**: Embrace the journey rather than focusing solely on the end result. Celebrate every small

win and recognize that growth happens gradually.

Final Thoughts

Change is challenging, but it's also an invitation to transform. By accepting and welcoming change, we develop a deeper resilience and open ourselves up to a richer, more rewarding life. Remember, the more you resist change, the harder life becomes. But when you lean into it with a growth mindset, you'll find yourself equipped to face any challenge life throws your way. Embrace change, step out of your comfort zone, and discover the transformative power of a life lived with openness and adaptability.

Embracing change isn't just about survival—it's about thriving. So, take that first step out of your comfort zone, and let your growth mindset guide you to the limitless possibilities that await.

Chapter 17

Consistency is the Game: Play it Daily

In the journey of personal and professional growth, consistency is the ultimate game-changer. It's not about the occasional burst of energy or a temporary high of motivation. Instead, it's about showing up every single day, whether you feel like it or not. Consistency is what transforms small efforts into lasting habits, and ultimately, into success.

As someone who deeply values self-improvement, I've seen firsthand how playing the game of consistency has shaped my life. Whether it's in my daily meditation practice, nurturing my passion for dance, or building meaningful connections with people, consistency has always been at the heart of my progress. Each day is a step forward, no matter how small, and these small steps accumulate over time, leading to significant transformation.

But the moment you stop playing this game, distractions and setbacks start creeping in. It's easy to deviate from your goals when you're not consistent. That's why consistency needs to be treated as a daily commitment—just like brushing your teeth or eating your meals. It's a non-negotiable part of life, especially when you have big dreams and aspirations.

Take my journey in image consulting, for example. The nervousness I felt during my first presentation wasn't a barrier—it was a signpost, pointing to areas where I could grow. Each weekend session added layers to my learning, making me more refined and confident. Similarly, my daily meditation practice helps me stay grounded, allowing me to manage thoughts and emotions, creating a clear, focused mindset.

Consistency also played a significant role in my dance journey. Starting Kathak later in life was a dream reborn, and despite the challenges, I've consistently pursued it, feeling a sense of fulfillment with each practice. The joy comes not from reaching a destination but from the process itself, from playing the game daily and knowing that every effort counts.

In both personal development and professional life, consistency builds momentum, resilience, and confidence. It's the game that brings you closer to your goals and aligns your actions with your vision.

So, let's commit to playing this game daily. Let's stay consistent, keep showing up, and remember that progress happens one small step at a time.

Chapter 18

The Power of Small Steps: How the Compound Effect Transforms Your Life

In today's fast-paced world, we often seek quick fixes and instant gratification, overlooking the true path to success—consistent, small steps that compound over time. This is the essence of the *Compound Effect*, a concept introduced by Darren Hardy in his book, which emphasizes the power of daily habits to create life-altering results.

About 15 months ago, I decided to implement a few simple practices into my daily routine:

- 5 minutes of meditation
- 15 minutes of reading
- 10 minutes of writing
- 30 minutes of dance as exercise
- 10 minutes of affirmations
- 5 minutes of visualization

- 5 minutes of gratitude

At first, these seemed like small, insignificant tasks. Five minutes here, ten minutes there—would it really make a difference? But I stayed committed, day after day, allowing these small actions to become part of my life. Now, over a year later, the results are astonishing.

Building Self-Confidence and Self-Esteem Each of these habits contributes to my overall growth. For example, spending 10 minutes daily on positive affirmations and 5 minutes on visualization has greatly enhanced my self-confidence and self-esteem. These practices allow me to focus on my strengths, align my mindset with my goals, and visualize success. This mental shift has had a profound impact, helping me approach challenges with a sense of belief in my abilities.

Raising Happiness Through Gratitude A simple act of spending 5 minutes daily on gratitude has been transformative. It has raised my happiness levels and shifted my perspective toward the positive aspects of life. No matter how small, acknowledging the good things around me has created a sense of contentment that I carry throughout the day.

The Power of Dance for Physical and Mental Well-Being Dancing for 30 minutes each day has not only improved my physical fitness but also uplifted my mood. This form of exercise brings joy, boosts my energy, and keeps me engaged with my body in a way that's fun and fulfilling. It's become a time where I not only take care of my health but also unwind and celebrate movement.

The Magic of Small Steps and Self-Discipline The magic lies in how these small steps have compounded over time. What initially required effort and planning has now become second nature. These habits have transformed into a daily routine that requires no motivation to maintain—it's simply part of who I am. This is the power of the Compound Effect. Small, consistent actions over time lead to monumental results.

Beyond just self-improvement, this process has also strengthened my self-discipline. By showing up every day, regardless of how small the task, I've trained myself to stay committed and focused. These small wins build on each other, creating a sense of accomplishment that motivates me to keep going.

The Takeaway What I've learned over the past 15 months is that progress doesn't always come from making big changes overnight. It's the accumulation of small, positive habits that lead to lasting transformation. Whether it's 5 minutes of meditation, 30 minutes of dance, or 5 minutes of gratitude, these small actions, when done consistently, create a ripple effect in your life.

So, if you're looking for change, don't underestimate the power of small, daily actions. Stick with it, trust the process, and watch as the Compound Effect unfolds—bringing confidence, happiness, and success into your life.

Chapter 19

Aligning Life with Nature's Phases for a Healthier and Happier You

When I was sitting in my meditation today morning this is what came, and I was inspired to write this.

Just as our day is divided into 4 Pahars (phases), our entire life unfolds in 4 Awasthas (stages). Nature has designed these phases with purpose, yet modern life often pulls us away from these natural rhythms, leading to imbalance and suffering.

- **Morning Pahar = Childhood (Baal Awastha)**

Just like the morning signals the start of the day, childhood marks the beginning of our journey. It's the time to awaken, learn, and build a strong foundation.

- **Midday Pahar = Youth (Yuva Awastha)**

As the sun reaches its peak, so does youth. This is the phase of energy, growth, and building our life's path. Yet, many of us, in the name of modernization, ignore essential habits and values that guide this powerful phase.

- **Afternoon Pahar = Adulthood (Praudh Awastha)**

Like the sun lowering in the afternoon, adulthood is the time for wisdom, stability, and reflection. It's when we should be reaping the fruits of our actions.

- **Night Pahar = Old Age (Vridha Awastha)**

As night falls, old age settles in. This is the time for rest, peace, and spiritual alignment, just as the night prepares us for the next cycle.

Today, I see people straying from these natural phases, letting modern habits and the **"Chalta Hai"** attitude govern their lives. This is bound to create problems, chaos, and a future filled with regret. Our **Sanatan Dharm** holds the key to aligning ourselves with nature. Everything is so clearly written in our holy texts. Even if we follow a small part of it, we can live a healthier, happier, and more fulfilling life.

Let's return to these ancient principles and live in harmony with the 4 phases of the day and life.

Chapter 20

The Power of Mind, Body, and Soul Alignment: A Journey to Holistic Health

For the longest time, I heard people say that the mind, body, and soul need to work in harmony to lead a healthy life. I used to dismiss it as just another piece of common wisdom—something people say but don't truly live by. Today, I understand it deeply, not just in theory but through my own experiences. If any part of this trio is neglected, life feels out of balance, leading to constant frustration, blame, and even diseases. What I now realize is that true health is holistic—**it's about nurturing your body, calming your mind, and connecting with your soul.** Here's how I've transformed my life.

Body: The Foundation of Physical Well-Being

Your body is the vessel that carries you through life, and taking care of it should be a top priority. Here's what I've incorporated into my daily routine:

1. **Proper Sleep**: A good night's sleep is non-negotiable. Without it, both your body and mind will suffer.

2. **Hydration**: Keeping your body hydrated is essential for maintaining energy and overall health.

3. **Mindful Eating**: Don't overstuff your stomach. Eating small, balanced meals at regular intervals has improved my digestion significantly. As I often say, when your digestive system functions properly, your mind is more at peace. You can see a similar theme in the movie *Piku,* where gut health is linked to mental clarity.

4. **Movement**: Moving your body daily is crucial. For me, dancing for about an hour each day has not only kept me physically fit but also helped me stay energized and positive.

5. **Gut Health**: I cannot emphasize enough how vital a healthy digestive system is. A well-functioning gut brings peace of mind and joy. It's one of the reasons why I feel happier and more in tune with life.

Mind: The Engine of Thought

Your mind is the source of your thoughts, and managing it is essential for leading a balanced life. Here's what works for me:

1. **Meditation and Reiki**: Both practices have been game-changers in maintaining my inner peace and fostering self-healing. I've been practicing Reiki healing for some time now, and it has truly helped me center myself.

2. **Reading**: Surround yourself with knowledge that uplifts you. I make it a point to read books that focus on personal growth and development, which consistently help me evolve.

3. **Positive Company**: I consciously choose to be around people who are non-toxic and add value to my life. Who we surround ourselves with plays a significant role in our mental well-being.

4. **Listening to Uplifting Audios**: Whether it's podcasts, audiobooks, or motivational talks, I've found that listening to the right content can raise my vibrations and shift my mindset.

Soul: The Core of Spiritual Strength

Finally, connecting with the soul is the **deepest form of self-care**. It's about nourishing your inner being and finding strength in spirituality:

1. **Prayer and Mantras**: Every morning and night, I pray and chant mantras to connect with my deity. This practice grounds me and provides inner strength, reminding me that the **Universe** works *for* me, not *against* me.

2. **Gratitude**: Practicing gratitude is a powerful tool that many underestimate. When you acknowledge the blessings in your life, you start to draw happiness from within rather than seeking it from external sources. It's a subtle but profound shift.

3. **Faith in the Universe**: Through consistent prayer and gratitude, I've developed a strong belief that when you're aligned with your higher self, the universe conspires to help you.

The Power of Thoughts

Our thoughts shape our reality. If you can control your thoughts, you can control your life. Over the past year, through these practices, I've been able to observe my thoughts more clearly. This self-awareness has benefited me immensely, both in my professional and personal life. I am at peace with myself, and that peace is reflected in every aspect of my life.

Conclusion

These practices have been life-changing for me, and I encourage everyone to try them. When you integrate care for your body, mind, and soul into your daily life, the transformation is undeniable. You begin to live a life of peace, purpose, and positivity. Consistency is key, and I promise, if you stick with it, the changes will amaze you. It's a game-changer. Give it a try—you won't regret it.

Chapter 21

G Savers: My Daily Mantra for a Better Life

Every day, I follow a powerful routine that has truly transformed my life—**G Savers.** These seven practices are my foundation for a more balanced, joyful, and productive day.

❖ **Gratitude**: I start each morning by acknowledging the blessings around me. It keeps me grounded and positive.

❖ **Silence**: Taking a few moments to be still helps me center my mind and recharge my energy for the day.

❖ **Affirmations**: Positive self-talk boosts my confidence and sets the tone for a successful day ahead.

❖ **Visualization**: I picture my goals vividly, allowing myself to align my actions with my dreams.

❖ **Exercise**: Keeping my body active with regular movement gives me the strength and focus I need.

◈ **Reading**: I feed my mind with knowledge, ensuring I continue growing both personally and professionally.

◈ **Scribing**: Journaling my thoughts, ideas, and reflections helps me stay clear on my journey.

Incorporating these practices into my daily routine has helped me improve my overall well-being, productivity, and mindset. I encourage everyone to give it a try—small, consistent steps lead to big changes!

How do you start your day? Let's uplift each other in this journey of self-improvement!

Chapter 22

The Alchemy of Self-Investment: A Transformative Journey

Throughout our lives, we often hear about the virtues of **self-investment** and continuous learning. The wisdom in these practices is universally acknowledged, yet it's easy to overlook their profound impact until one embarks on the journey personally. Over the past year, I've delved into the art of self-investment, and the metamorphosis has been nothing short of alchemical.

At first, the concept seemed abstract—a nebulous idea, often discussed but rarely explored in depth. However, as I committed to this path, I began to witness a transmutation within myself. The day I decided to invest in my growth, everything shifted. It was as if a dormant potential within me had been awakened, catalyzing a profound transformation.

The most remarkable change has been the emergence of a new persona—a more fortified, resilient version of myself. This isn't just about acquiring new skills or knowledge; it's about fostering an inner equilibrium that permeates every aspect of life. There's a newfound tranquility, a sense of harmony that resonates both internally and externally.

What's truly enchanting about this process is its subtlety. The changes are not always immediate, but they are cumulative and deeply ingrained. Each step in the journey adds another layer to your being, gradually crafting a stronger, more robust self. It's akin to the process of forging steel—the intense heat and pressure are necessary to create something enduring and powerful.

If you have yet to embark on this journey of self-investment, I implore you to begin now. The rewards are not merely tangible but also deeply intrinsic. The outcome is indeed magical, a testament to the power of deliberate, continuous self-improvement. It's an alchemical process that has the potential to reshape not only your life but also your very essence.

In a world that often emphasizes external achievements, investing in oneself remains the most potent and transformative act of all. It's an investment that yields the greatest return—a stronger, wiser, and more peaceful you.

Chapter 23

The Power of Desire

Losing my father at the age of 8 left a void that no amount of love or support could fill. My mother, though a pillar of strength, couldn't replace the unique bond that a father provides. This loss left me with low self-esteem and a deep sense of loneliness, which shadowed me throughout my formative years. Yet, even in those early days, something within me resisted the notion that my worth was tied to anyone's expectations or perceptions.

As I navigated through life, challenges frequently arose, often in the form of words meant to diminish me. "Why worry? You won't have to work after marriage," an elder who was like a father figure once told me. I didn't respond; I simply let the words settle into the quiet corners of my mind, knowing they did not define me.

As I grew older, the challenges didn't diminish; they merely evolved. When I expressed an interest in a career in sales, I was met with skepticism. "You won't succeed in sales," they said. This time, the words stung a bit more, yet I chose silence again—not out of agreement, but because I understood that the only response that mattered would be my actions.

These instances were not isolated. Even as a child, I was labeled "absent-minded" simply because I didn't answer a relative's question. I wasn't being inattentive; I was just lost in my thoughts, contemplating the world in my own way. Again, I chose not to argue or defend myself. Instead, I kept moving forward, driven by a quiet yet powerful force within me.

Now, at 40, I stand proud of the person I've become. I've defied every expectation that sought to limit me. With over 14 years of professional experience, I've not only succeeded in sales but have also been recognized as a top performer. Beyond my career, I've grown spiritually and mindfully, achieving a balance and fulfillment that many seek but few find.

Through all these life experiences, I've learned a fundamental truth: People will throw stones at you in the form of words, trying to diminish your worth. But what truly matters is how you see yourself—your perception of your own value. Your **self-image is crucial**, and it's not something others can define for you.

Reaching this level of self-assurance and resilience wasn't easy. It required significant inner work, a **relentless belief** in my potential, and most importantly, an **unwavering desire to succeed.** This is the **power of desire:** It's a force that ignites within you, pushing you forward when the world tries to hold you back. It's that fire in your belly, that deep-rooted belief that you are capable of more than anyone can imagine.

Desire is the fuel that drives you to overcome obstacles, to silence the naysayers, and to achieve your dreams. It's the force that transforms adversity into strength, silence into action, and doubt into confidence. With desire, anything is possible.

So, I urge you to keep fueling that desire. Let it guide you, empower you, and remind you that you are capable of achieving greatness. The rest, as they say, will become history.

Chapter 24

Be the Driver of your own Life!!

Why taking charge of one's life is important?

Being the driver of your life is crucial for numerous reasons, and here are five key points highlighting its importance:

1. Personal Empowerment and Autonomy:

- Taking control of your life empowers you to make decisions that align with your values, goals, and aspirations. This autonomy fosters a sense of ownership and responsibility, leading to greater confidence and self-efficacy.

2. Goal Achievement and Fulfillment:

- When you steer your own life, you can set clear, meaningful goals and take deliberate actions to achieve them. This proactive approach increases the likelihood of fulfilling your personal and professional aspirations, leading to a more satisfying and purposeful life.

3. Resilience and Adaptability:

- Being the driver of your life enables you to navigate challenges and uncertainties more effectively. By actively making choices and adapting to changing circumstances, you build resilience and the ability to overcome obstacles, rather than feeling helpless or victimized by external factors.

4. Alignment with Authentic Self:

- Taking charge of your life allows you to live authentically, making choices that reflect your true self rather than conforming to others' expectations or societal pressures. This alignment with your genuine desires and values leads to greater happiness and inner peace.

5. Improved Relationships and Influence:

- When you are in control of your life, you can establish healthier boundaries and communicate your needs and intentions more clearly. This leads to stronger, more respectful relationships and enhances your ability to positively influence and inspire others, both personally and professionally.

Chapter 25

Letting Go | An Art

When did **YOU** learn the art of letting go?

Last week, an incident forced me to do some self-introspection. My younger daughter, who is in 3rd grade, was supposed to address the assembly at her school. It was Tuesday morning, and her assembly date was scheduled for Thursday, so we were in preparation mode. But here's the twist: we received a call that morning informing us the assembly was actually scheduled for Tuesday itself. Panic ensued, but since my patience has improved through meditation, I was able to control the situation and reassure her that she had practiced the night before and could handle it. She went to school.

When she returned home, I asked her while giving her food what happened in the assembly. Very candidly, she said, "I forgot." My expression was one of shock, eyes wide open and body language full of disbelief. I asked her what happened next. She said, "My principal scolded my class teacher, my class teacher scolded me, and then I scolded my friend."

Her spontaneous answer made me burst into laughter, and I was rolling on the floor laughing.

I asked her if she felt bad, and she said, "Yes, a little bit, but what can be done? What's done is done." When she uttered these words, it struck a chord in me. I realized that children are so sorted in their feelings and that we should learn from them. They are the best teachers and can teach us important lessons about emotions. This conversation touched me deeply, and I was happy that she knew how to let go of things, which many of us struggle with, leading to various issues in our lives.

It's always important to leave the baggage of the past behind and move forward to see what the future holds for us. For me, it was a revisited lesson in letting go and finding solutions during challenging times.

www.ingramcontent.com/pod-product-compliance
Lightning Source LLC
LaVergne TN
LVHW041626070526
838199LV00052B/3257